D0640753

Heather
2013

Endpapers - photograph by Frank Whitney, courtesy TIB®

Interior photos courtesy Image Bank:
Page 6 - Graduation Cap & Diploma © G.K. & Vikki Hart;
Page 11 - Columns, Washington, D.C. © MCMXCIV
David W. Hamilton; Page 18 - Capitol Bldg., Montgomery,
Alabama, Columns © MCMXCII - Flip Chalfant; Page 25 -
Columns of Federal Building/Alabama © LXXXIX Nick
Nicholson; Page 26 - Still Life Column/Pedestal ©
MCMXCI Antonio M. Rosario; Page 32 - Columns
Concept: Stability, Strength, Support © Stuart Dee;
Page 39 - Roman Column © MCMXCIII Hans Neleman;
Page 46 - Middle East - Palmyra, Syria © MCMXCVII
Carolyn Brown; Page 51 - Roman Column © MCMXCIII
Hans Neleman; Page 63 - Graduation Cap and Diploma
© MCMXCIV - Tim Jonke

Congratulations

ON

YOUR

GRADUATION

Contents

Follow
Your Dreams

Go for the moon. If you don't get it, you'll still be heading for a star.

Willis Reed,
quoting one of his
high school coaches

I don't believe in planning for the future. I believe in planning for now.

Ray Charles

Anybody can start something.

John A. Shedd

The best way to predict the future
is to invent it.

Alan Kay

Even if you are on the right track,
you'll get run over if you just sit
there.

Will Rogers

My mother drew a distinction between achievement and success. She said that "achievement is the knowledge that you have studied and worked hard and done the best that is in you. Success is being praised by others and that's nice, too but not as important or satisfying. Always aim for achievement and forget about success."

Helen Hayes

The only way to discover the limits of the possible is to go beyond them into the impossible.

Arthur C. Clarke

Even a fool knows you can't touch the stars, but it doesn't stop a wise man from trying.

Spoken by Harry Anderson,
Night Court (TV sitcom)

Action is eloquence.

William Shakespeare

Growth is the only evidence of life.

Cardinal Newman

We need objectives. We need focus and direction. Most of all, we need the sense of accomplishment that comes from achieving what we set out to do . . . it's important to make plans, even if we decide to change them, so that at least for the moment we know where we're going and we can have a sense of progress.

Leon Tee

It takes a certain level of aspiration before one can take advantage of opportunities that are clearly offered.

Michael Harrington

The future belongs to those who believe in the beauty of their dreams.

Eleanor Roosevelt

You may be disappointed if you fail, but you are doomed if you don't try.

Beverly Sills

As we acquire more knowledge, things do not become more comprehensible, but more mysterious.

Albert Schweitzer

Life is a series of experiences, each one of which makes us bigger, even though it is hard to realize this. For the world was built to develop character, and we must learn that the setbacks and griefs which we endure help us in our marching onward.

Henry Ford

One day at a time—this is enough. Do not look back and grieve over the past, for it is gone; and do not be troubled about the future, for it has not yet come. Live in the present, and make it so beautiful that it will be worth remembering.

Ida Scott Taylor

Every calling is great when greatly pursued.

Oliver Wendell Holmes, Jr.

It is the true nature of mankind
to learn from mistakes, not from
example.

Sir Fred Hoyle

Use missteps as stepping stones
to deeper understanding and
greater achievement.

Susan L. Taylor

Flaming enthusiasm, backed up
by horse sense and persistence, is
the quality that most frequently
makes for success.

Dale Carnegie

You cannot create experience. You
must undergo it.

Albert Camus

Believe in Yourself

I approach the future in a happy
and rather adventuresome spirit.
It is within my power to make
this unknown path a somewhat
beaten path.

Paul Robeson

The world is divided into people
who do things and people who
get the credit. Try, if you can, to
belong to the first class. There's
far less competition.

Dwight Morrow

In ourselves are triumph and
defeat.

> *Henry Wadsworth Longfellow*

Integrate what you believe in
every single area of your life. Take
your heart to work and ask the
most and best of everybody else,
too.

> *Meryl Streep*

The shortest answer is doing the
thing.

> *Author unknown*

To accomplish great things we must not only act but also dream, not only plan but also believe.

Anatole France

The roots of true achievement lie in the will to become the best that you can become.

Harold Taylor

The thing always happens that you really believe in, and the belief in a thing makes it happen.

Frank Lloyd Wright

Never let the fear of striking out
get in your way.

George Herman "Babe" Ruth

What great achievement has been
performed by the person who
told you it couldn't be done?

Melvin Chapman

Get action. Seize the moment.
Man was never intended to
become an oyster.

Theodore Roosevelt

Every great work, every great accomplishment, has been brought into manifestation through holding to the vision, and often just before the big achievement, comes apparent failure and discouragement.

Florence Scovel Shinn

Confidence begets confidence.

Proverb

Things are only impossible until they aren't.

Spoken by Captain Jean Luc Picard,
Star Trek: The Next Generation

I was successful because you believed in me.

Ulysses S. Grant

Optimism is the faith that leads to achievement. Nothing can be done without hope and confidence.

Helen Keller

We are what we repeatedly do. Excellence, then, is not an act, but a habit.

Aristotle

A human being is only interesting
if he's in contact with himself. I
learned you have to trust yourself,
be what you are, and do what you
ought to do the way you should
do it. You have got to discover
you, what you do, and trust it.

Barbra Streisand

Do the hardest thing in the world
for you. Act for yourself. Face the
truth.

Katherine Mansfield

Action is the proper fruit of
knowledge.

Thomas Fuller

To be nobody but yourself—in a world which is doing its best, night and day, to make you everybody else—means to fight the hardest battle which any human being can fight, and never stop fighting.

e. e. cummings

Let me tell you the secret that has led me to my goal. My strength lies solely in my tenacity.

Louis Pasteur

You must be the change you wish
to see in the world.

Mohandas K. Gandhi

Keep away from people who try
to belittle your ambitions. Small
people always do that, but the
really great make you feel that
you, too, can become great.

Mark Twain

You can't do anything about the
length of your life, but you can do
something about its width and
depth.

Evan Esar

Look inside to find out where
you're going . . .

*The Artist formerly
known as Prince*

Don't be afraid to take a big step.
You can't cross a chasm in two
small jumps.

David Lloyd George

I may not have gone where I
intended to go, but I think I have
ended up where I intended to be.

Douglas Adams

Faith can give us courage to face
the uncertainties of the future.

Martin Luther King, Jr.

When you want something, go
back and go back and go back,
and don't take no for an answer.
And when rejection comes, don't
take it personally. It goes with the
territory. Expose yourself to as
much humiliation as you can bear,
then go home and do it all again
tomorrow.

Betty Furness

Learn Whatever You Can, Wherever You Can, from Whomever You Can

One looks back with appreciation to the brilliant teachers, but with gratitude to those who touched our human feelings.

Carl Jung

Education is what survives when what has been learned has been forgotten.

B. F. Skinner

I have always worshipped at the shrine of knowledge knowing that regardless of how much I study, read, travel, expose myself to enriching experiences, I still remain an intellectual pauper.

Adam Clayton Powell, Jr.

I not only use all the brains that I have, but all that I can borrow.

Woodrow Wilson

The empires of the future are the empires of the mind.

Winston Churchill

Man, unlike any other thing
organic or inorganic in the uni-
verse, grows beyond his work,
walks up the stairs of his con-
cepts, emerges ahead of his
accomplishments.

John Steinbeck,
Grapes of Wrath

A man should keep his little brain
attic stocked with all the furniture
that he is likely to use, and the
rest he can put away in the lum-
ber room of his library, where he
can get it if he wants it.

Arthur Conan Doyle

Don't be afraid to give up the good to go for the great.

Kenny Rogers

Success is that old ABC —ability, breaks, and courage.

Charles Luckman

Education is the ability to listen to almost anything without losing your temper or your self confidence.

Robert Frost

The greatest revolution in our generation is that of human beings, who by changing the inner attitudes of their minds, can change the outer aspects of their lives.

Marilyn Ferguson

It ain't enough to get the breaks. You gotta know how to use 'em.

Huey P. Long

Go around asking a lot of damfool questions and taking chances. Only through curiosity can we discover opportunities, and only by gambling can we take advantage of them.

Clarence Birdseye

An expert is someone who knows some of the worst mistakes that can be made in his subject, and how to avoid them.

Werner Karl Heisenberg

Make all you can, save all you can, give all you can.

John Wesley

I am not afraid of storms for I am learning how to sail my ship.

Louisa May Alcott

The greatest discovery of my generation is that a human being can alter his life by altering his attitudes of mind.

William James

anytning with-
out getting in someone's way. You
can't be detached and effective.

Abba Eban

Success is to be measured not so
much by the position that one has
reached in life as by the obstacles
which he has overcome while
trying to succeed.

Booker T. Washington

Minds are like parachutes—they
only function when open.

Thomas Dewar

There is only one success— to be
able to spend your life in your
own way.

Christopher Morley

I think the one lesson I have
learned is that there is no substi-
tute for paying attention.

Diane Sawyer

Experience is not what happens
to a man. It is what a man does
with what happens to him.

Aldous Huxley

At my old school there is at least one teacher who loves me. She is the teacher who "knew me before I was born" and bought my first baby clothes. It is she who makes life bearable.

Alice Walker

The best careers advice to give to the young is "Find out what you like doing best and get someone to pay you for doing it."

Katherine Whitehorn

To know the road ahead, ask
those coming back.

Chinese proverb

Get the advice of everybody
whose advice is worth having—
they are very few—and then do
what you think best yourself.

Charles Stewart Parnell

The only way to enjoy anything in
this life is to earn it first.

Ginger Rogers

I find that a great part of the information I have was acquired by looking up something and finding something else on the way.

Franklin P. Adams

Live neither in the past nor in the future, but let each day's work absorb your entire energies, and satisfy your widest ambition.

Sir William Osler

This Is Just the Beginning

The fireworks begin today. Each diploma is a lighted match. Each one of you is a fuse.

Edward I. Koch

If A is a success in life, then A equals x plus y plus z. Work is x; y is play; and z is keeping your mouth shut.

Albert Einstein

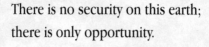

There is no security on this earth;
there is only opportunity.

Douglas MacArthur

If we value the pursuit of knowledge, we must be free to follow
wherever that search may lead us.
The free mind is no barking dog,
to be tethered on a ten-foot chain.

Adlai E. Stevenson

Try to put into practice what you already know; and in so doing, you will, in good time, discover the hidden things which you now inquire about. Practice what you know, and it will help to make clear what now you do not know.

Rembrandt van Rijn

To the being fully alive, the future is not ominous but a promise; it surrounds the present like a halo.

John Dewey

Love of learning is seldom
unrequited.

Arnold H. Glasow

The greatest accomplishment is
not in never falling, but in rising
again after you fall.

Vince Lombardi

Luck to me is something else:
hard work—and realizing what is
opportunity and what isn't.

Lucille Ball

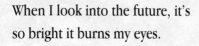

When I look into the future, it's
so bright it burns my eyes.

Oprah Winfrey

If you reach for the stars, you may
not quite get them, but you won't
come up with a handful of mud
either.

Leo Burnett

There is a very real relationship, both quantitatively and qualitatively, between what you contribute and what you get out of this world.

Oscar Hammerstein II

Everybody knows if you are too careful you are so occupied in being careful that you are sure to stumble over something.

Gertrude Stein

Hope for the best. Expect the
worst. Life is a play. We're unre-
hearsed.

Mel Brooks

I like the dreams of the future
better than the history of the past.

Thomas Jefferson

Man's mind, once stretched
by a new idea, never regains its
original dimensions.

Oliver Wendell Holmes, Jr.

Tomorrow is the most important thing in life. Comes in to us at midnight very clean. It's perfect when it arrives and it puts itself in our hands and hopes we've learnt something from yesterday.

John Wayne

It is wise to submit to destiny.

Chinese proverb

Education is the one peaceful technique for creating changes for the better.

Howard H. Brinton

I must admit that I personally measure success in terms of the contributions an individual makes to her or his fellow human beings.

Margaret Mead

Wisdom lying dormant is like an unproductive treasure.

Arabic proverb

I don't know the key to success, but the key to failure is to try to please everyone.

Bill Cosby

Every addition to true knowledge
is an addition to human power.

Horace Mann

Nobody promises you a good
time or an easy time. I don't know
who it was who said when we
think of the past we regret and
[when] we think of the future we
fear. And with reason. There are
no bets on it. There is the present
to think of, and as long as you
live, there always will be. In the
present, every day is a miracle.

James Gould Cozzens

To improve the golden moment of
opportunity, and catch the good
that is within our reach, is the
great art of life.

Samuel Johnson

Mix a little foolishness with your
serious plans: it's lovely to be silly
at the right moment.

Horace

Declare the past, diagnose the
present, foretell the future.

Hippocrates

Knowledge may give weight, but
accomplishments give lustre, and
many more people see than
weigh.

Earl of Chesterfield

Perhaps the best thing about the
future is that it only comes one
day at a time.

Dean Acheson

The supreme accomplishment is to blur the line between work and play.

Arnold Toynbee

You really *can* change the world if you care enough.

Marian Wright Edelman

If you can react the same way to winning and losing, that is a big accomplishment. That quality is important because it stays with you the rest of your life.

Chris Evert

The future is not something we enter. The future is something we create.

Leonard I. Sweet

The bird that flies out of the ashes . . . will rise from the ashes on new wings.

Judy Collins

Don't worry if you can't do the best thing every time—you'll rob yourself of the enjoyment of the things you *can* do.

Barbara Cawthorne Crafton

Never mistake motion for action.

Ernest Hemingway

With a bit of courage and a dash
of self-discipline, a small talent
can go a long, long way.

Kitty Carlisle Hart

Let us run with endurance the
race that is set before us . . .

Hebrews 12:1